Sports Illustrated KIDS

Mascot Mania

BASEBALL'S WACKIEST MASCOTS:

FROM BILLY MARLIN TO THE PHILLIE PHANATIC

BY DAVID CARSON

Published by Capstone Press, an imprint of Capstone.
1710 Roe Crest Drive North Mankato, Minnesota 56003
capstonepub.com

SPORTS ILLUSTRATED KIDS is a trademark of ABG-SI LLC. Used with permission.

Library of Congress Cataloging-in-Publication Data
Names: Carson, David, 1973- author.
Title: Baseball's wackiest mascots : from Billy Marlin to the Phillie Phanatic / by David Carson.
Description: North Mankato, Minnesota : Capstone Press, 2023. | Series: Mascot mania! | Includes bibliographical references. |
Audience: Ages 8-11 | Audience: Grades 4-6 | Summary: "A fuzzy, green creature is spotted dancing with fans on top of the Philadelphia Phillies' dugout. Crew members chase after a wacky chicken on the San Diego Padres' field. A mischievous seal is caught trying to steal the San Francisco Giants' home plate-literally! Baseball fans love to watch and applaud the playful antics of colorful mascots. Join the fun and learn all about the wackiest baseball mascots!"-- Provided by publisher.
Identifiers: LCCN 2022013097 (print) | LCCN 2022013098 (ebook) | ISBN 9781666353136 (hardcover) | ISBN 9781666353099 (pdf) | ISBN 9781666353112 (kindle edition)
Subjects: LCSH: Baseball--Miscellanea--Juvenile literature. | Sports team mascots--Juvenile literature.
Classification: LCC GV867.5 .C374 2023 (print) | LCC GV867.5 (ebook) | DDC 796.357--dc23/eng/20220509 LC record available at https://lccn.loc.gov/2022013097 LC ebook record available at https://lccn.loc.gov/2022013098

Editorial Credits
Editor: Aaron Sautter; Designer: Terri Poburka; Media Researcher: Morgan Walters; Production Specialist: Polly Fisher

Associated Press: Charles Krupa, spread 10-11, Mike Carlson, 23, Rich Kane, spread 8-9; Getty Images: Carmen Mandato, 25, Dylan Buell, 20, Jamie Sabau, 26, Mark Brown, 19, Sean M. Haffey, 12, Stephen Dunn, 17; Shutterstock: shaineast, top right 5, Stockagogo Photos, soread 4-5; Sports !llustrated: Al Tielemans, spread 6-7, spread 14-15, Damian Strohmeyer, Cover, Erick W. Rasco, Cover, John Biever, top right 21, spread 28-29, John W. McDonough, Cover, Robert Beck, Cover

All internet sites appearing in back matter were available and accurate when this book was sent to press.

Table of CONTENTS

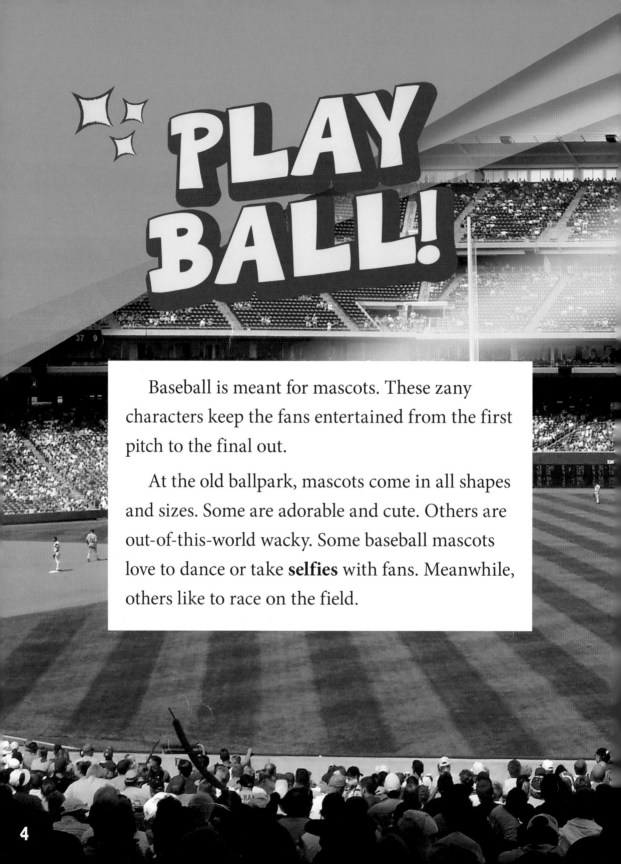

PLAY BALL!

Baseball is meant for mascots. These zany characters keep the fans entertained from the first pitch to the final out.

At the old ballpark, mascots come in all shapes and sizes. Some are adorable and cute. Others are out-of-this-world wacky. Some baseball mascots love to dance or take **selfies** with fans. Meanwhile, others like to race on the field.

Baseball parks are home to some famous mascots. Some are old-school legends like The San Diego Chicken or the Phillie Phanatic. Other mascots are newer to the scene like Clark the Cub or Wally the Green Monster. Whether old or new, baseball mascots keep the fans entertained at the ballpark.

THE PHILLIE PHANATIC

He's big. He's green. He's furry. He's the Phillie Phanatic!

The Philadelphia Phillies' mascot may be the most famous in all of baseball. But what is it? With googly eyes and a funny snout, the Phanatic is a mystery. Some say he's a sort of flightless bird from the Galapagos Islands.

Whatever the Phanatic is, one thing is certain—he's a whole lot of fun! He skydives. He ziplines. He zooms around the field on his four-wheeler between innings. Not to mention his famous **dugout** dances. There's nothing the Phanatic won't do to entertain the crowd.

Did You Know?

The Phillie Phanatic is also famous away from the ballpark. He's often appeared on TV shows such as *The Simpsons* and *The Goldbergs*.

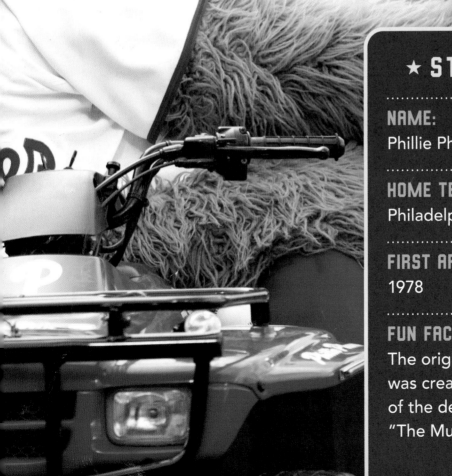

★ STATS ★

NAME:
Phillie Phanatic

HOME TEAM:
Philadelphia Phillies

FIRST APPEARANCE:
1978

FUN FACT:
The original Phanatic was created by one of the designers for "The Muppets."

MR. MET

Nothing says baseball quite like Mr. Met. He has a giant baseball head, after all. Mr. Met first appeared in 1963. With that giant smile and fun-loving spirit, it didn't take long for him to become a fan favorite in the Big Apple. Mrs. Met joined Mr. Met at the stadium in the 1970s to root on their favorite team.

Mr. Met loves to "high four" the fans at Citi Field, the Mets' home stadium. He also loves hanging out with his younger fans and snapping selfies with them at the stadium's Kiddie Field.

WHAT'S IN A NAME?

The Mets first joined Major League Baseball (MLB) in 1962. Their official name was the New York Metropolitan Baseball Club. This was in honor of the New York baseball team from the late 1800s. But their name was soon changed to "The Mets" that we know today.

★ STATS ★

NAME:
Mr. Met

HOME TEAM:
New York Mets

FIRST APPEARANCE:
1963

FUN FACT:
Mr. Met was Major League Baseball's first modern, live-action mascot.

WALLY THE GREEN MONSTER

Be careful if you ever visit Boston's Fenway Park. You might find a monster! But this monster isn't scary. Far from it. Wally the Green Monster is the loveable mascot for the Boston Red Sox.

Fenway Park is one of the oldest ballparks
in the Major Leagues. Perhaps its most unique
feature is the left field fence. The wall stands
37 feet (11.3 meters) tall. It's no wonder the left
field wall is nicknamed "The Green Monster."

Legend says that Wally the Green Monster has
lived behind the giant left field fence since 1947.
But he stayed out of sight and remained a secret.
Finally, he emerged in 1997 to show himself to
the world. He's been a fan favorite ever since.

THE SAN DIEGO CHICKEN

The San Diego Chicken is a true **trailblazer** in the wacky world of mascots. The Chicken is famous for his zany on-field stunts. He also loves to poke fun at opposing players and coaches. And he can't resist a classic "pie in the face" **prank**. But it's all in good fun, and the fans love it.

The Chicken got his start at the San Diego Zoo in the mid-1970s. A few years later the kooky rooster began appearing at San Diego Padres games. His big, floppy feet, goofball appearance, and wacky antics quickly made him a fan favorite.

The Chicken's popularity soon stretched beyond San Diego. Over the years, the Chicken has made appearances everywhere from the White House to WrestleMania.

THE BASEBALL BUNCH

During the 1980s the San Diego Chicken appeared each week on a children's TV show called "The Baseball Bunch." Kids loved watching the Chicken's wacky skits. Meanwhile, baseball legends like Johnny Bench and Tommy Lasorda gave coaching tips for young players watching at home.

★ STATS ★

NAME:
San Diego Chicken

HOME TEAM:
San Diego Padres

FIRST APPEARANCE:
1974

FUN FACT:
For more than 50 years, the Chicken has been played by only one person, Ted Giannoulas.

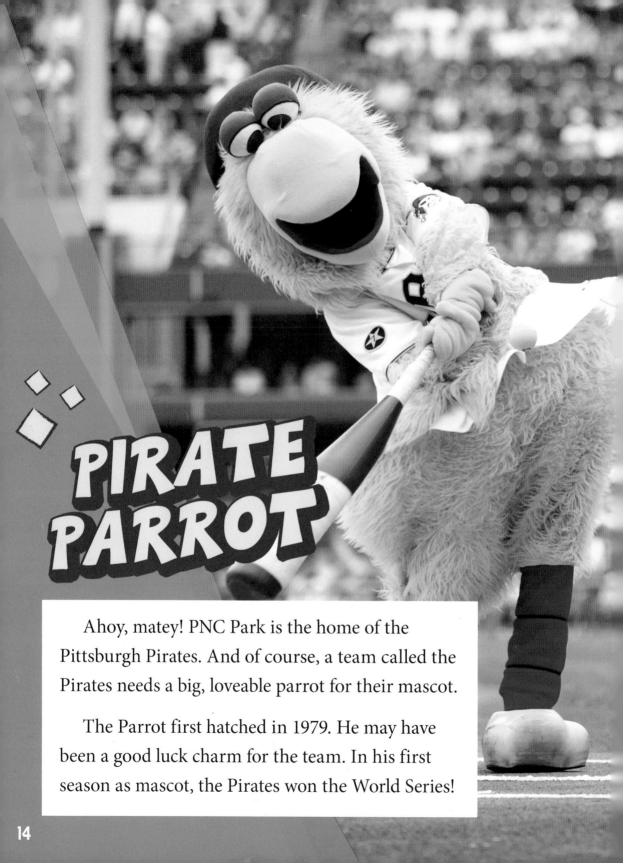

PIRATE PARROT

Ahoy, matey! PNC Park is the home of the Pittsburgh Pirates. And of course, a team called the Pirates needs a big, loveable parrot for their mascot.

The Parrot first hatched in 1979. He may have been a good luck charm for the team. In his first season as mascot, the Pirates won the World Series!

The lime green, fuzzy bird can't be missed in the stadium. Over the years, the Parrot has changed a lot. He's gotten taller, heavier, and goofier looking. During games, the Parrot loves to dance, dance, dance. And he never turns down a chance to take a selfie with his young fans.

Did You Know?

Major League Baseball's championship is called the World Series. The first World Series took place in 1903 when the Boston Americans beat the Pittsburgh Pirates.

★ STATS ★

NAME:
Pirate Parrot

HOME TEAM:
Pittsburgh Pirates

FIRST APPEARANCE:
1979

FUN FACT:
According to official stats, the Parrot averages 121.6 high fives per game.

LOU SEAL

Lou is one cool seal! He's always wearing his hip sunglasses and backward baseball cap. A mascot as cool as Lou loves taking selfies with his fans. He can even be seen kayaking in McCovey Cove outside the ballpark.

When not entertaining his fans, Lou lives in the icy waters underneath Lefty O'Doul Bridge. For Lou, it's just a short swim to Oracle Park to cheer on his Giants. On gameday, Lou loves to hang out with his younger fans. He also makes regular appearances at birthday parties and charity events around San Francisco.

Did You Know?

San Francisco's original baseball team was called the Seals. It was one of the best minor league teams in the early 1900s. Baseball legends Joe DiMaggio and Vernon "Lefty" Gomez both played several seasons for the Seals.

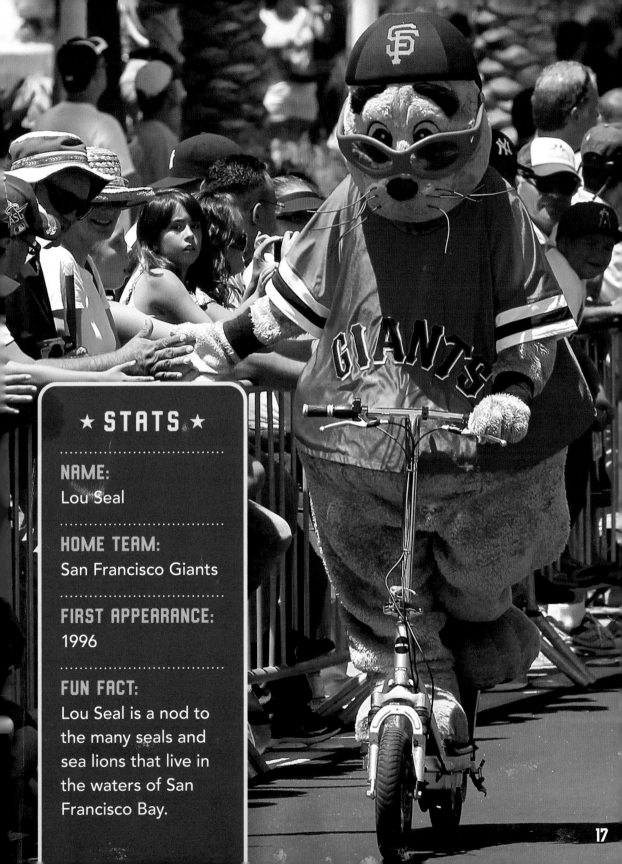

★ STATS ★

NAME:
Lou Seal

HOME TEAM:
San Francisco Giants

FIRST APPEARANCE:
1996

FUN FACT:
Lou Seal is a nod to
the many seals and
sea lions that live in
the waters of San
Francisco Bay.

BILLY MARLIN

There's something fishy going on in southern Florida. It's Billy the Marlin! This oversized, funny fish has been entertaining fans at Miami Marlins' home games since 1993.

Billy's got big googly eyes, a long **bill**, and a huge smile. Billy loves hanging out in the Fan Zone, an area in the stadium designed for family fun. Selfies and wacky dancing are just part of the game for Billy.

The fifth inning of each home game is Billy's time to shine. That's when he competes in the regular water boat race. Marlins fans love this crazy video race that's shown on a large screen in the outfield.

Did You Know?

Billy's name is based on the fact that marlins are a type of "billfish." Other billfish include sailfish and swordfish. All billfish have long spear-like "bills" they use to swipe at **prey**.

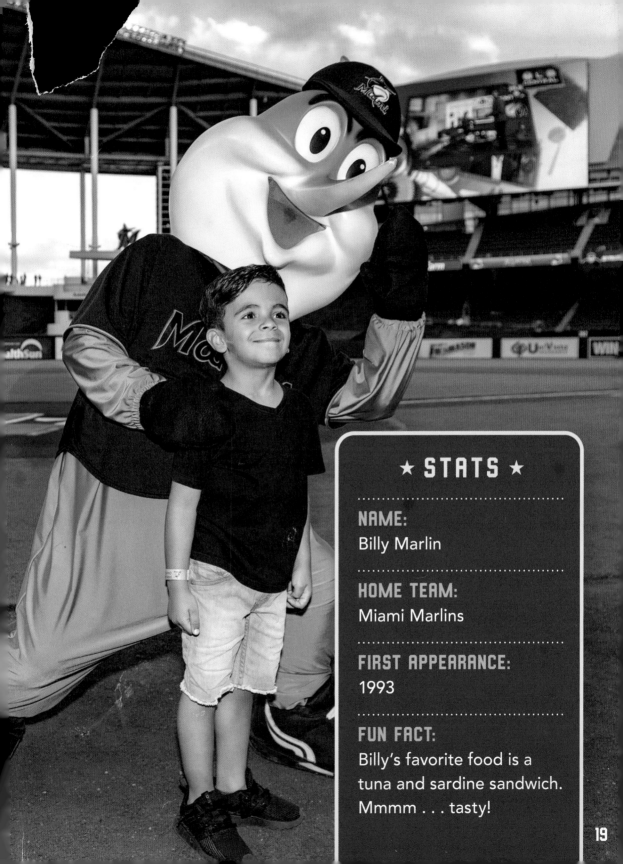

★ STATS ★

NAME:
Billy Marlin

HOME TEAM:
Miami Marlins

FIRST APPEARANCE:
1993

FUN FACT:
Billy's favorite food is a
tuna and sardine sandwich.
Mmmm . . . tasty!

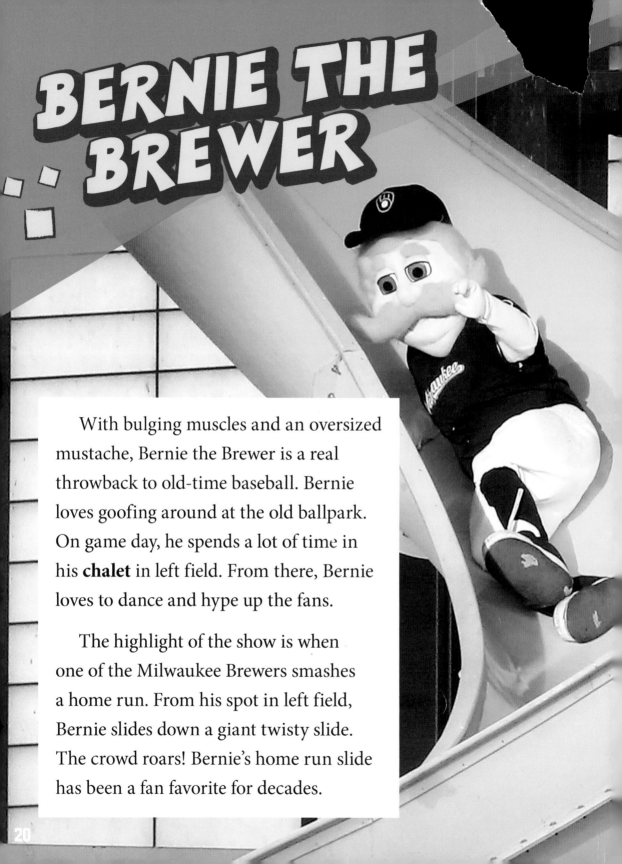

BERNIE THE BREWER

With bulging muscles and an oversized mustache, Bernie the Brewer is a real throwback to old-time baseball. Bernie loves goofing around at the old ballpark. On game day, he spends a lot of time in his **chalet** in left field. From there, Bernie loves to dance and hype up the fans.

The highlight of the show is when one of the Milwaukee Brewers smashes a home run. From his spot in left field, Bernie slides down a giant twisty slide. The crowd roars! Bernie's home run slide has been a fan favorite for decades.

RACING SAUSAGES

Bernie the Brewer isn't the only costumed fun during Brewers' games. Before the seventh inning at each home game, the crowd gets to cheer for their favorites in the Great Sausage Race. Several lucky fans get picked for the race. They put on oversized sausage costumes and compete in a hilarious foot race on the field. Each wacky costume represents the delicious food Milwaukee is famous for: a bratwurst, Polish sausage, Italian sausage, hot dog, and **chorizo**.

★ STATS ★

NAME:
Bernie the Brewer

HOME TEAM:
Milwaukee Brewers

FIRST APPEARANCE:
1973

FUN FACT:
Bernie's likeness is modeled after a diehard Brewers fan from the 1970s.

STOMPER

Stomper might be a scary name, but he's a gentle giant. With his big floppy ears and an adorable snout, even the littlest fans love Stomper.

Why is an elephant the mascot for the Athletics? It all started as a private joke between two team owners in the early 1900s. Ever since then, the image of an elephant has been part of the team. But it wasn't until 1997 when Stomper finally joined the team as the official mascot.

During home games, Stomper throws t-shirts to the crowd. But his favorite thing is taking selfies with his younger fans. When not at the stadium, Stomper is active in the city. He loves appearing at birthday parties, parades, and charity events around Oakland.

★ STATS ★

NAME:
Stomper

HOME TEAM:
Oakland A's
(Athletics)

FIRST APPEARANCE:
1997

FUN FACT:
Stomper can throw a baseball with both hands.

ORBIT

Orbit is the out-of-this-world mascot for the Houston Astros. He's green. He's furry. He's an alien with a silly grin stretching from **antennae** to antennae.

Orbit has come a long way to be a Big League mascot. He was born all the way out in Foul Territory of the Grand Slam Galaxy. He first arrived on Earth in 1990 to cheer on his favorite team.

Astros fans love Orbit's zany antics. He loves to break out his t-shirt gun and launch **souvenirs** into the crowd. This crazy alien also can't resist pulling pranks on the opposing team. Even the players love interacting with Orbit on the field in-between the action. But Orbit's favorite activity is the dance party that follows most home games.

★ STATS ★

NAME:
Orbit

HOME TEAM:
Houston Astros

FIRST APPEARANCE:
1990

FUN FACT:
Orbit loves to dance.
What's his favorite move?
The moonwalk, of course.

CLARK THE CUB

Win or lose, there's always one Cubs fan with a big smile on his face. Clark the Cub has been the happy-go-lucky mascot for the Chicago Cubs since 2014.

In just a few years Clark has become one of the most favorite mascots in all of sports. He looks cool hanging around Wrigley Field with his backwards ballcap, sunglasses, and oversized Cubs jersey.

Before games Clark is often spotted outside the stadium taking photos with the fans. Once the game gets started, Clark loves to lead the crowd in singing "Go, Cubs, Go!" The team's official song always gets the stadium rocking!

★ STATS ★

NAME:
Clark the Cub

HOME TEAM:
Chicago Cubs

FIRST APPEARANCE:
2014

FUN FACT:
Clark is the "grandbear" of Joa, a live bear that was the Cubs mascot way back in 1916.

Did You Know?

Clark gets his name from Clark Avenue, a famous street where Wrigley Field is located.

DINGER THE DINOSAUR

Dinger is the adorable mascot for the Colorado Rockies. He's a purple dinosaur with a great big smile. The area around the Rockies' home stadium is well-known for dinosaur **fossils**.

In 1994, workers found some pieces of dinosaur bones while building the stadium. The find gave team owners an idea. Soon after the stadium opened, Dinger the Dinosaur hatched right on the field. The Rockies had their first mascot!

Dinger loves dancing behind home plate to distract the visiting team. It may not always work, but the fans love their favorite Dino's zany pranks.

Did You Know?

Many fans wanted to name the Rockies' stadium "Jurassic Park" after the classic dinosaur movie.

★ STATS ★

NAME:
Dinger the Dinosaur

HOME TEAM:
Colorado Rockies

FIRST APPEARANCE:
1994

FUN FACT:
Dinger gets his name for the baseball slang term for a home run.

GLOSSARY

antennae (an-TEN-ee)—feelers on some creatures' heads used for sense and touch

bill (BIL)—a long, spearlike snout found on some kinds of fish

chalet (sha-LEY)—a small house or cottage

chorizo (chuh-REE-zoh)—a spicy sausage often used in Mexican cooking

dugout (DUHG-out)—a low shelter that holds the players' bench; baseball fields have one dugout for each team

fossil (FAH-suhl)—the remains or traces of an animal or a plant, preserved as rock

prank (PRANGK)—an amusing trick played on someone for fun

prey (PRAY)—an animal hunted by another animal for food

selfie (SEL-fee)—a photograph that is taken by the person who appears in it, usually with a smartphone or other digital camera

souvenir (soo-vuh-NEER)—an object kept as a reminder of a person, place, or event

trailblazer (TREYL-bley-zur)—a person who is the first one to do something

READ MORE

Berglund, Bruce. *Baseball GOATs: The Greatest Athletes of All Time.* North Mankato, MN: Capstone Press, 2022.

Doeden, Matt. *G.O.A.T. Baseball Teams.* Minneapolis: Lerner Publications Group, 2021.

Gale, Ryan. *Military Animal Mascots.* Minneapolis: ABDO, 2021.

INTERNET SITES

Mascot Hall of Fame
mascothalloffame.com

Major League Baseball
mlb.com

Sports Mascots
sportmascots.com/mlb/

INDEX

ABOUT THE AUTHOR

David Carson is a photographer and freelance writer. He's been a sports fan all his life and loves to root on his favorite MLB team, the Chicago Cubs.